THE BAD WINTER

THE BAD WINTER

JAMES CROWDEN

FLAGON PRESS

2008

First published 2008
By Flagon Press
Whitelackington
Designed by Andrew Crane
Typeset in Monotype Baskerville
Printed in Milborne Port by Remous Ltd

A CIP record for this book is available
from the British Library
ISBN 978-0-9557073-6-0

The cover photograph
is reproduced with kind permission of the
Western Morning News.

These poems are dedicated to all those
who have worked on the moor in adverse
conditions and in particular to the memory of
Zacharias Pascoe and George Bowden.

CONTENTS

INTRODUCTION

This collection of poems has a historical narrative running through it. Some of the poems evolved out of conversations many years ago, others are more recent. In particular the memories of such people as George, Ethel and David Bowden, Fred and Don Peek and the farmers around Meavy left a deep impression on me as a child. Although I was brought up in Tavistock, my mother's parents lived in Meavy. My parents were married there, I was christened there and both my grandparent's funerals were held there. It was and still is an important village to me, for it contains my earliest memories. My grandmother's first cousin was a writer called Winston Graham and his books on Cornwall and Poldark took pride of place on the bookshelves in the White Cottage. So for me there also was an early attraction to writing. My grandfather, Captain Henry Moulton, who sang in the church choir for many years, had been in convoys in both wars and so there was a strong link to the sea as well as to the moor. The Royal Oak also played its part.

Only relatively recently have I delved into the life of Zacharias Pascoe. When I mentioned his name to Dr Tom Greeves in Tavistock he exclaimed "Not THE Zacharias Pascoe?" Indeed it was the same man that Tom knew from his tin mining research. Zacharias is an interesting antecedent to have on one's side in times of trouble. In 1800 his daughter Jane Pascoe married a quarterdeck gunner Dennis Crowden who had recently come into a good wodge of prize money from the capture of two Spanish frigates heavily laden with gold, silver and drugs from South America.

When I grew up in Tavistock the snow and arctic conditions of the 'Bad Winter' of 1962-63 left a very deep impression on me and maybe it is no coincidence that I later spent a winter in the Himalayas.

Dartmoor is endlessly evolving and it is the working men and women who live on the moor that fascinate me. These poems are only a start but I hope that they give some insight into the conditions on the moor, as well as the ancient history that lies just under the surface.

James Pascoe Crowden 2008

ACKNOWLEDGEMENTS

I am very grateful for the help given to me to by Dr Tom Greeves of Tavistock, to Dr Peter Addyman for allowing me on his archaeological dig at Lydford all those years ago, to David Bowden of Meavy for retracing the stories of his parents George and Ethel Bowden, also to Arthur Smith and Rupert Hill for interviews about the bad winter. To Robert Trevelyan for helping me to locate the cover photograph and to the Western Morning News for allowing me reproduce it. To Carol Trewin and Guy Crowden for proof reading, Catherine Simmonds for consultancy and Andrew Crane for design and to Remous Ltd for printing.

THE MOOR

When you have been brought up on the moor,
Weaned on wind, thick mist, low cloud and freezing rain,
The elements tease out your inner sense of direction,
Navigation honed down between heather and bracken,

The maze of narrow winding, sheep tracks
Imprinted on early memory,
The granite compass set firm within your bones,
Old seams worked out, your skin a glistening sheen

Flecked with quartz and lichen, capped off with sedge
And cotton grass, drinking from a cupped hand,
The school of rivers and streams flowing from your eyes,
Soft dark peat that melts between your fingers,

Sucks you in, fathom by fathom, until only your head
And shoulders show above the belly of the mire,
And then your words hover,
Words that are heard faintly on the lips of the wind,

Words that slowly die away as the moor
Swallows you whole, till there is nothing left
But the reedy, fluty song of skylarks
Spiralling up from your finger tips.

THE BAD WINTER 1962-63

THE COLDEST PROLONGED WINTER SINCE 1740

1. That year winter tightened its fist upon the land,
Laid siege to the prison,
Snuffed out a few thousand sheep
And in a twinkling wrote off a handful of Morris Minors.

Snow and black ice took their toll
The land's clock stopped dead, icicles came home
To roost, suspended in their own solidity.
Old trains equipped with snow ploughs, mysteriously

Vanished overnight, swallowed up by Siberian snowdrifts
And never to be seen again farmhouses were battened down.
Every morning the rime on the windows ran riot
Like maps of underwater currents, icy ferns that grew

Of their own accord, a crystal world unfolding
As you watched, then before breakfast,
The rime scraped off with your fingernails.
Snow creaked underfoot, sheep became icebergs,

Rivers became glaciers. Arctic on your doorstep
Polar exploration, a distinct possibility.
Muffled silence became addictive,
Spring wound back to zero. Even the sea froze.

2. Slowly we learnt to exercise our new found
Freedom and ventured further afield,
Laws of gravity were explored.
Maps now had crevasses, avalanches were common,

Vast snowballs gathered pace downhill.
Rotund white statues dotted the landscape.
It took a while to get used
To the beginnings of speed,

Ice out of control, mercilessly catapulting you
Down what was once the main road
On makeshift toboggans, tin trays
Or old plastic fertiliser bags,

A hint of rebellion that lasted for months.
There was talk of an emergency
But nothing much happened, except the breathing
In of cold air, the dazzle of sunlight.

Snow and silence interlocked, school cancelled
And like Zen monks we entered a closed order,
Went up to the moor, observed its pale face,
A vast moon upon which we walked, slowly like small gods.

3. Three months we had of it in all,
Windblown drifts as tall as a house.
People brought out their cross-country skis,
Talked of dog teams racing in the Yukon.

Shades of Eskimo Nell and Desperate Dan McGrew.
Cars and land rovers had chains strapped
Around their wheels that skidded and rattled in the ruts.
Ponies came down to the cattle grids to be fed

And farmers went out with long poles
In search of lost sheep in the lee of walls,
Digging down into the whiteness if they sensed
The warm of breath, igloos snugly encased in ice.

Sometimes they survived for weeks,
Miraculously living off their fleece and thin air.
Helicopters delivered bread and hay.
The prisoners were doubly trapped.

No appeal. No remission for good behaviour.
One farm cut off for thirteen weeks.
It left its mark, that winter, a point of reference,
A yardstick that can still be brought out and dusted down.

BLIZZARD

We heard the last train go through
Rattling over the iron bridge,
As it crossed the Tavy at a slight angle
Steam engine chuntering to itself.

There was something odd about the snow
You could not quite put your finger on it,
It came down fast and silent as if from nowhere
Heavy flakes from a darkening sky and went on for days.

It had no respect for railway timetables or platform tickets
Shovels were all they had to hand, whole trains
Encased in ice as fires were let down gently and pistons froze,
The joy of steam condensing on the inside.

The white overcoat which cooled the boilers, shunted the track
Into a siding as the sharp wind drove the drifts,
Powered the white buffers, dragged men from their beds,
Grasped their wooden hands and did not let go.

CHILDE'S TOMB

They found him curled up
Frozen in the belly of his horse,
Foxtor Mire, no place for a merchant
In a blizzard, wind sharp as a raven's beak,

But sensible for all that, he somehow scribbled a note
To whoever might find him first,
Burial instructions that galvanised at least
One abbey into unprecedented action.

The horse, however had a raw deal
Throat and belly slit, a last ditch attempt to stay alive,
The warmth of blood and entrails,
A strange cloak - wolf fodder. They built a bridge.

TAVISTOCK ABBEY CIRCA 996 AD

Ordulph made me, a Benedictine hall house
Of prayer for Our Lady and St Rumon, the Breton prince
Whose sacred bones have made many cures miraculous
An abbey glittering in the gloaming
A jewel set beside the fast flowing river
A place of God on this, the wilder side of the moor
A frontier between speech and looks
Language and longings, ideas forged in the King's metal
A storehouse endowed with books and chalices
A token of worship, a place of beauty
A stone cross carved beneath the trees
A crossing place, a bridge between two worlds
Endowed, the future state, God's kingdom, a cloth woven in gold
Obedience, loyalty to this, the new crown, the crown of thorns
A jewel as fair as Elfrida who now sleeps with the king
Elfrida whose beauty has already cost the life of Athelwold
Elfrida sister of Ordulph, sister-in-law of Aelfwynn
Ordulph son of Ordgar, now brother-in-law to King Edgar
Such is the ancestry, the line that laid the foundation,

God's pasture, a simple chant, early in the morning
Candle guttering, devotion, the hours of obedience
A new fealty, fostered and fuelled, a favourite spot
Beside the water, the litany of life's passage
The power beyond kneeling and prayer
Messages of forgiveness and subservience,
The land's sovereignty committed to the coffers,
Count house and still house,
The ledger of reckoning, the hide's gesture
The litany of grain, mutton, wool, salmon, eel and goose
Cattle, swine, ale and herbs, remedies down by the river,
The scribe's legacy, manuscripts, lodged and illuminated
Glittering with gold and vermilion, the riddles of the moor
Streamed and brought down for assay and coinage
Ancient rights farmed out, a small paradise tucked away,
An abbey richly endowed, ripe for picking.

ARCHAEOLOGY – THE LYDFORD PENNY

The Anglo Saxons had me on my knees for weeks on end
In penitent April showers, excavating post holes, the sites
Of wooden houses, a small trowel, round wooden handle,
Fits neatly into the palm, short stubby blade worn down.

The only solace in bad weather, midday lunch at the Inn,
Washing odd fragments of reddish pottery, the finds shed.
But the Lydford penny was as elusive as ever in Silver Street,
Liquid history smelted, stamped out, siezed by the Vikings

Coins of the realm, the raids a rough and ready package holiday.
Events well chronicled, original broadsheet still survives.
Danegeld in mint condition, images of Aethelred and Canute
Harold and Edward the Confessor still turn up in Gotland.

The Baltic hideaways. Swedish oarsmen a thirsty lot.
Now under tarmacadam, the village car park,
Well defended, the gorge, a dark throat that swallows
Its own history, bleak castle in keeping with its own laws.

Within the ramparts molehills move, an Anglo Saxon riddle
That we never quite solved, silver roots of our own language
Flourishing deep within rich shadows, earthy stories hang in mid air,
Sentences weave between the trees, frontier zone for the watch keeper.

TAVISTOCK MARKET c 1498

Good business down there in Tavistock
Those monks know how to look after themselves
Why a quarter of wheat fetches eight shillings
And two quarters will get you an oxen
There's eight to a team mind
So two oxen's the same as a hundredweight of wool
Hard work that is, shearing I mean
Only a penny a score,
And not gone up in two hundred years
Everything else went up after the Black Death
Why shepherds and ploughboys get the same now
Gone from 3d a week to 8d
If you are lucky with food thrown in.
And look what's happened to the price of wool
Since they started tinkering with it,
All that weaving on the continent,
Shouldn't be allowed
That's what I say,
And you got to watch the weights and measures.

The Exeter Bushel is not the normal 8, but 10 gallons
And a rod is not 16 feet, but a generous 18
And a hundredweight not 112 but 120 lbs
Everything is on the generous side
Except the Duchy, the King's tax
Swiped at source, half a crown a hundredweight
For tin to get the stamp, diluting coinage,
To pay the troops in France, an old trick.
Why the silver from Bere Alson,
Helped financed two crusades.

And a hide, a season's plough?
Officially of course, it is 120 acres
And a quarter hide, a virgate,
And a quarter virgate, a ferling
If you follow me,
Which makes a ferling about 7 acres.

But then in Devon, a ferling may be
Anything from 15 to 32 acres
The sort of area a family could live off
A unit of survival more or less
With a bit of wood and pasture thrown in
And rights between dawn and dusk
Which makes you wonder
What a hide must have been.

But then in Cornwall they're even more generous
A Cornish acre is anything
From 15-300 English acres,
So you can choose which side of the river
You'd rather be born.

Me? I'm off to buy some geese.

Pigeons you say?
Pigeons are a penny a brace
Do you want some?
Or is it a sheep you're after?
Sheep's better at scavenging
Than a cow on the moor

You're lucky if you get two stone of cheese a year
Tis only three sheep to the cow
When it comes to milking
That's if they stay alive over winter
What with scab, murrain and starvation.

So being realistic for a moment
Pigeons is awful dear
Why a penny is the same as mowing
Half an acre of his lordship's meadow
Or one day's ploughing,
But when it comes to reaping
Two acres is 4d
Or to put it another way
Three geesé in lieu.

But if you want something interesting to do
Fish is where it's at
Nice clean salmon,
No net marks, 1/3d at the Abbey
Lent, a godsend.
No meat on the animals anyway
But don't get caught,
They own the fish weirs
But stay clear of deer
You'll end up in Lydford.
Food for crows,
Hung drawn and semi-slaughtered.
Not a nice sight.

Geese is what I'm after, and then
I'll shove a few more cattle on the moor
Nobody'll notice
Then it is tin, I know a good spot,
But I can't tell you where, just yet
Unless of course you got some readies up front,
And a way of bypassing
The Lord Warden of the Stannaries.
You see if you get caught
They make you swallow molten tin
Uncomfortable they tell me
And difficult to swallow.
But if it's work you want
All sweat and rabbit stew
I'm your man! Going far?

NEXT SPRING

When the ice cap melted
You found sheep bones and tufts of wool
Picked up skulls and compared horns.

Anatomy on a vast scale,
Vertebrae glistening, divination
An easy matter, the autopsy

Played out time and time again
Picked clean, the pale shoulder blade
And jaw bone, teeth rattling

Musty smell of death still lingering
A place of uncertainty
Black cattle and escaped convicts.

ZACHARIAS PASCOE 1749-1843

Wild card, tin streamer, riot man, ancestor,
Sluicer of rocks and leatsman, chewer of mountains,
Heather and tobacco, eats peat before breakfast
Reads the dew in the palm of his hand, pans for tin
On the end of his shovel, takes to the moor like an otter,
Clouds slung over his shoulder, brings contours to heel,
Ingenuity within his grasp, leads water across hillsides
A sheaf of silver threads that glisten to his bidding
With launders, wheels and sluices, each small tributary
Engraved on his ruffled brow, mining for stories,
Elusive ore that runs through the earth's muscle
The adit of knowledge passed on down,
The punch of granite, a bible of rock, each pitch and lode
Chapter and verse, a rich vein brought to surface.

CHAGFORD TINNERS' RIOT
– THE WILD WEST: 1793

That November morning Zachary Pascoe and his Cornish mates
Came down off the moor, legged it into Chagford, took the tinners' law
Into their own hands. They only wanted fair play, to rescue two
Of their own who had strayed into drink and riotous behaviour.

But wrecking was in their blood. They surveyed the narrow streets
And cargoes in the cellar, as if a foreign ship had come ashore.
Reckoned three weeks was all it would take to level a town
The size of Chagford, a precise art, recycling and reclamation.

Skilled workmen used to estimating pitches, lodes and levels
Handling black powder, the short fuse, tribute underground.
But caution was thrown to the wind that day as they marched upon
The town, a noisy rabble with cudgels hidden beneath their coats.

The friends they sought, spirited away, hung over, locked up.
The motley crew tailed six miles or more till they came close
To the Magistrate's house, thought better of the militia's muskets,
That evening, cooled their heels in Exeter Bridewell. Basic B&B

But the miners had a trump card, bringing tin and copper ore to grass.
The war with Napoleon fresh about their ears. Straining at the leash,
And released without charge, their pride intact, they legged it back home.
Zachary stayed another fifty years upon the moor, rather liked it.

LEAT

Sure footed, reliable
Confident in its own destiny
Silver thread that runs for miles

Skirts the tor, leads the eye
Down to farms and old mine workings
Driving wheels and pumps

Crazing mills and Cornish stamps
Man-made brooks that babble
To themselves, carry stories off the moor.

MOOR RAIN

Rain is what Dartmoor does well
Shedding the fleece as neatly
As the Pennines,

Vertical then horizontal
Pummels the wool till it clings
Around the neck, a ruff of felt.

The only shelter
Lee of a dry stone wall
The intake of breath.

GRANITE

Tempered by the wind
Granite has its own tonality
Stretched out across the moor

Landmarks that quarry the sky,
Etched memorials,
Shivering faces, grey islands,

As lonely as Tierra del Fuego
In the mist, constellations adrift
Embedded within sheeps' consciousness.

CHINA CLAY

Decayed·granite, old feldspar
Surprising in the south,
Once conical mounds
That shimmered under moonlight

Gave guidance to German bombers
Were covered in turf
And camouflage nets
Long before Christo was around.

Deep pits that yawn are now blasted
With high pressure hoses, monitors
Pumped and then settled out
The soft feel of kaolin - deep pools of azure blue,

Spawn white rivers that once reached
Down to the China Sea.
Glossy magazines and Cookworthy
Lapsang - one sugar or two?

FICE'S WELL

Circle of granite
Shrine to water
Entrapping the quietness
Of the moor,

Images of fern reflected
In Blackabrook's babble
The small clapper
Discreet but useful,

The land half tamed
Brought back in hand
The couple
Bewitched by mist.

FRENCH PRISONERS ON THE MOVE
24TH MAY 1809

A breath of fresh air that fine May morning, the forced march
Inland from foetid hulks in the Hamoaze, men from *Le Brave, El Firm,*

Yan Sidro, San Nicholas, Hector, exercising old muscles, escort militia
With fixed bayonets, a French invention fresh from Bayonne.

Le Caton, Genereux, long bedraggled lines with wagons and carts
That straggles out across the moor, *L'Oiseau, Bien Faisant, San Pareil*

A millipede that crawls towards grey walls, Frenchman's Road.
The only port of call, stone frigates that hold men's lives in the balance…

They must have heard the skylarks rising, caught a glimpse of sea
Aired hammocks before stout doors clanged shut behind the granite arch.

'Parcere Subjectis', Virgil calling out to us. 'Spare the vanquished'
They found their own level, out on parole or gambling in the cockloft.

Les Lords, Les Indifferents, Les Laborieux, Les Minables,
And last of all *Les Romains*, naked, feral, 'hatchers of mischief'.

The officers of course went hunting or courted the local ladies
Danced and made advances, while others carved delicate miniatures

Turned mutton bones into sleek ships of the line, imprisoned in bottles,
The rigging, strands of cotton, sailing before the mast on a glassy sea,

Time whittled away, old stories unpicked, Madame Guillotine,
For the chop, bone idle, caulking below the water line, bartered, gambled,

Sold for food and baccy. Napoleon's war tucked behind bars.
They played Breton tunes, cursed the English cooking.

How they must have longed for home, clean clothes, French skirt.
Those vessels outlived their makers, still sail on in my imagination.

PASCOE'S WELL

By the wall, a faint run with a ditch nearby
Just out of sight of the prison

A clump of beech trees
You might pass without even realising

That a cottage once stood here.
He may even have planted the trees himself.

Snug, Pascoe's Well tucked in under
Slender granite slabs beside the road

More ferns and a foxgloves
Few if any ever stop to look.

Another small shrine to clear water
Half silted up, but useful in summer droughts

And in the very depths of winter
When all else was frozen hard

The well kept its composure
Made itself very useful.

PASCOE'S COTTAGE

Zacharias settled here, encroached
His own patch, was allowed to stay.

No man's land. The year after Trafalgar
Built the cottage with his own hands

Sandwiched between Maristow and the Duchy.
The estate map shows the cottage clearly

Just down from Rundlestone
His name in running script, *Z Pascoe*

An oasis just below the prison leat
Dug peat, lived rough and ready.

With his stone mason sons
Four generations crammed under one roof

But Zacharias, Cornish to the last
Tin miner at ninety-two

Census tucked under his leather belt,
Dreamed of lodes and striking it rich

Looked west again beyond Wheal Lucky
The promised land on his doorstep.

CONVICTS ON THE MOVE

– HOLMING BEAM

Out of the mist, the daily migration
Long line of grey lags
Shuffling feet, averted eyes

Warders on horseback
Each with a carbine
Slung over the shoulder.

Return from tree planting, sentry duty
Regiments of green spiky soldiers,
Heeled in behind a granite wall

A blessing to get out of the wind
Sun a thin memory
The trudge of steps

Not a word amongst them.
The light failing
Each with their own plan of escape

Hatched out and rehearsed
A hundred times
Small habits that keep men sane

Dark secrets hidden in the peat
No shackles
Just the whiff of mailbags

Letters home
Each one written in invisible ink
Sentences trailing off into the distance.

PEAT CUTTING

Out at the tie he laid the turves bare
Wet and glistening, the low bank
Straightened up to his bidding

Explored the soft darkness
With a long, narrow iron
That dug into the peat

Each cut a thin slice laid out
Like small black bibles, history
Waiting to be read, the resurrection

Stacked up in small stooks, warmth
Gleaned from the neck of the moor
Carried home on the wind's saddle.

SWALING AT ERME PLAINS

I watched him from a safe distance
As he dismounted then crouched down

On one knee in the trough of the moorland
A solitary figure, his back turned and bent

Rough tweed jacket and leather gaiters
Blended in, reins thrown over the horse's neck

As he deftly played with fire,
And let it run where he wanted.

At first he did not notice me,
But I watched him for a full five minutes

Before he turned, put his foot in the stirrup
And regained the well-worn saddle

Not a word did the quarter man speak
Yet we both marvelled at his handiwork

A ritual offering to bring new grass
The smell of burning heather

The dry crackle and blue smoke
Running smoothly like a bolt of silk

Between his fingers
Towards the row of standing stones.

DITSWORTHY WARREN

As George walked to school across the moor
The smell of skinned rabbits lingered on his fingers.

Two miles each way whatever the weather,
Keeping his cousin Percy company.

He worked on the warren setting snares,
Trapping vermin, checking up on coney pillows,

Feeding hay in winter, the breeding cycle, endless rabbit runs,
And Old Lady Ware with the iron cooking pot over the open fire,

Comforting, the fragrant smell of peat smoke,
A homing beacon in the dusk.

The warren, a living city netted under moonlight
Like a river bed on the move, long nets staked out and dogs,

Legis Tor and Hen Tor as well, 1,000 acres more or less
You'd wring the rabbits' necks as fast as you could,

Deft flick of the wrist. The cold hours before dawn,
Then paunch them and hock them, pack them in hampers,

Pony and cart to the nearest railway halt, destined
For Liverpool and Plymouth. Skins once paid the rent.

GEORGE BOWDEN – MEAVY

1. Powder monkey, warren boy and stoker,
China clay worker and parish lengthsman
I remember him coming out of the woods
With an axe on his shoulder, kindling the light
Old hessian sack tied over his shoulders,
Another around his waist, a medieval apron.
His fingers crumpled up, knotted with arthritis,
A lifetime on the moor carved from the wind,
A keen blue twinkle still alight in his eye.
He walked gently, quietly down the rutted track
Across the open field and within that steady pace,
And wily gait, the granite jaw set against the sky,
A stubborn independence, the like of which
You'll rarely see again. The moor left its mark.

2. Often I heard the story about crossing the moor in winter
With Harry, his older brother, head keeper at Holne Chase
Keeping Christmas up at Sheepstor, they followed
The tracks into Huntingdon Warren, took a bowl
Of rabbit stew, then struck out into the snow again,
A dozen miles of open moorland, the Abbot's Way
And George only ten years old. The blizzard began to bite,
And all he wanted to do was to curl up, teeth chattering
And go to sleep in a snowdrift. But Harry kept nudging
Him on with the toe of his boot to keep him awake,
To keep him alive, then carried him high on his shoulders,
Like a sack of potatoes, half conscious, the last few miles
Touch and go for both of them, snow up to the knees,
Each drift deeper than the last. The blizzard left its mark.

3. After the warren, china clay out at Redlake,
The cream of Dartmoor taken in hand, dug out,
White mounds of sand and rock refined
Flexed his muscles, piece work, stripping overburden,
Blasting rocks and horse tramming. Long shorts
And hob nailed boots, maintaining dirty water leats
Keeping the face clean and free from peat, no easy task.
Then back to Lee Moor landing clay in the kilns,
The drying sheds. Warm work steamed out,
Long flick of the shovel, the clay like putty
Shipped down to the docks. Incline railways
From Wotter, steep track maintained, steel wire rope
Fast and efficient the mechanism down to Marsh Mills
Shifting the white burden. China clay left its mark.

4. When the First War reared its ugly head,
George chose the navy, signed on the dotted line
For the duration, shovelled coal below decks,
A County class cruiser stoked boilers
Coughed up black dust, the bunkers lethal,
Tons of coal unstable shifting on a whim,
More dangerous than a mine, saw men hammered
By red hot furnace doors swinging in a storm,
Chests and backs branded like a horse
Or scalded with steam. Bellville Boiler Jack,
Triple expansion engines, three funnels, two shafts,
Six inch guns. Every admiralty knot paid for
In shining sweat. Roast rabbit for Christmas.
Couldn't get away from them. Coal left its mark.

5. During the Second War they guarded the dam
Covered china clay tips in turves, the conical mounds
Under moonlight, dead give-away for Heinkels
En route for Plymouth and the dockyard,
The camouflage nets, streets ahead of Christo.
Then thirty years as parish lengthsman, his weapon of choice,
The long handled Devon spade to remove the dirt
And over burden, he knew the water tables
Keeping lanes and gullies clear, shovelling snow in winter
Sickle, stick and red flag, in summer, hedging,
A way of leaning into the cut. The bottle of cold tea
Moored in the shade. Odd jobs like Fernworthy Reservoir.
George liked the long tramp across the moor,
Inner freedom on his own terms. Silence left its mark.

YEO FARM

Above the arch, the year 1610, carved confidently
Into the granite, the farmhouse solid, stylish for those days,
Just up from the water splash and Marchant's Cross.

1610, the same year Henry Hudson sailed into Hudson's Bay
And Galileo found the moons of Jupiter. For three centuries
The farm ran on its own steam then was slowly cast adrift.

The First World War lived out day by day by as Ethel Smale
Waited for news of her brothers on the Western Front
And sweetheart George as he shovelled coal upon the Seven Seas.

Newspapers and casualty lists were hard to get.
No telephone. No radio. So towards the end, when rumours
Were rife, they arranged with Uncle Wally the signalman

At Dousland to get the engine driver on the Princetown line,
To give three long blasts of his steam whistle
On a certain bend before Burrator when they knew

For definite that war was ended and they were coming home.
How they jumped and danced and hugged and kissed
Each other in the kitchen that November day.

Years later when sheep were living in the house,
Floors were falling in and the moon shone through the roof
I could still sense their happiness, the whistle on the bend.

BURRATOR AT DUSK

Calm between pines, moss on boulders
Watery mirror reflecting night sky
The lake fractured, dark bands of cold deepness

Inverted moorland, hovering,
On the edge of consciousness
Keeping its own thoughts to itself.

Silent, the faint ripple, makes its own apologies
From hidden depths, where abandoned
Farmhouses and cottages have learnt to swim.

The old Sheepstor bridge, far below,
Its arch still in place, submerged, embalmed
Pointing in a different direction.

BURRATOR AND THE LUFTWAFFE – MAY 19TH 1941

The bomber came down unexpectedly
That Monday night, moon in the last quarter
Just missed the dam and reservoir
Ended up in Lowery marsh, a Junkers 88.

George Bowden and Harold Shillibeer,
Stalwarts of the Home Guard, rushed up to parapet,
Saw the flames, but could not save the crew.
Bits of one at least were found on Sharpitor. He'd lost a leg.

Their charred remains collected up and buried
Very close to where George was born.
Four small hummocks at the far end with wooden crosses
That we used to visit whenever we were passing.

True, they were giving Plymouth a pasting with incendiaries
But they must have been hit or way off course.
Maybe they thought they could get the dam as well.
The rush of water carrying all before it. Germany calling.

THE GARDEN NEXT DOOR
– SCRAP METAL

It was always there,
The rusty German helmet
From the First War
Hung upside down off the apple tree
A birdbath, a relic, a trophy
Of the trenches
Brought back by Jack Smale
The First War inverted.

And further along the path
Bits of Sherman tank,
Valances for the tracks
To keep the raspberries at bay.
No questions were ever asked
About his miraculous escape
Or where the tank bits ended up
The Second War purloined.

CAPTAIN HENRY – THE WHITE COTTAGE

1. When the time was right he unrolled the charts, and spread
The North Atlantic out on the long oak dining room table,
Half a fathom of linen backed cloth that still held its own secrets.
His ocean now becalmed and unruffled, annotated in red and green ink,
Longitude and latitude ingrained on his furrowed brow.
Deep in thought, the grandfather clock ticked quietly away to itself
As he showed us the convoy routes Liverpool-Reykjavik-Halifax.

Backwards and forwards hugging the pack ice, an escort agency
Chaperoning cargo vessels, old tramp steamers, oil tankers and trawlers,
Tugs and whaling ships. As navigator of the Armed Merchant Cruiser
He had to know exactly where they all were by dead reckoning
And the stars. Then he pointed to the Denmark Straits with the stem
Of his pipe 'Very unhealthy' he said with a wry smile, 'in March'
As the *Prinz Eugen* sailed through a smoke screen of Old Holborn.

2. He looked at the chart again, then pointed to other other locations.
The sister ship, the *Rawalpindi* sank in the Iceland Gap.
Ludovic Kennedy's father steering straight for a brace of battle cruisers,
On fire from stem to stern, only a handful survived. Then further south
The *Jervis Bay*, under Fogarty Fegan, outgunned again, this time
The *Admiral Scheer*, but the convoy scattered. Yes, he had good friends
In both, who went down with the ships. That was the expression he used.

It sounded genteel, serene, almost humane, but we knew that was
Not the case. He explained the importance of sighting reports and
Admiralty codes. Then one particular convoy. May '41 I think it was.
U boats. Nine ships went down, they had to steam through survivors,
Could not alter course. Men on fire jumping from ships.
Deep in thought the grandfather clock ticked away to itself
As Dartmoor sun came in through the window and Greenland melted.

LAST OF THE BLUE GRASS

At the front door of the cottage two Devon spades
Leaning against the wall, their long curved handles still intact

Heart-shaped shovels blunted by a lifetime's work
Balance just right for throwing dirt high up over the hedge.

One of the last men in the village with connections
To Sir Francis Drake, nephew of the more famous pirate,

"Captain art tha sleepin there below?
Slung a'tween the round shot in Nombre Dios Bay"

Buster waits for the social worker to fix the rota, check the pills.
Three phase never phased him, welder and electrician

They sent him to the Greek earthquake, Argostoli, 1953.
'You could still feel the aftershocks, the ground cracking up.

The cells crushed out of shape. Couldn't get the prisoners out,
So their solution was to pull a pin and throw grenades in.

That made me realise I had to mind my p's and q's.
Then a poor old soul was searching for her belongings in the ruins

Near to curfew time. The Greek militia never even challenged her,
The sentry just swung a sub-machine gun round and fired a burst.

When you are young, you are adversely affected by such things.
He had orders, I suppose, to stop the looting. Life's cheap out there.'

Buster played Blue Grass after the war, rode into the local town
On his Matchless with full blown Stetson and guitar strapped

Across his leather back. 'Buster Bowden and the Western Revellers.'
Up market hill-billy and for stage, gun belt, holsters and six-shooters.

Even played Dartmoor prison before Johnny Cash tried San Quentin.
Appalachian dance tunes still circle in Buster's head.

No doubt they will send a Spanish nurse next week from Cadiz
Or a request for him to join the bowls club on the Hoe

When all he wants is his 12 bore back and a little bit of rabbit shooting
'Father had a powder monkey's licence you know.'

At the front door two Devon spades their handles still intact
Heart-shaped shovels blunted by years of work, balance just right.

POSTMAN

Knowing every family he delivers milk
And food parcels to outlying farms

Takes confession by the roadside
Like a priest keeps his ear to the ground

Gauges each small community on his own barometer.
Passes on messages, who's ill, who's died,

Who's sheep have yet to be sheared
Who's courting who and when it is due.

Takes post to the prison by the sack load
The outside world for a thrupenny stamp

And knows full well when the wind is veering
To the north east and beckons snow,

White tunnels etched on his memory
Drifts piled high above his van windows

Digging his way back round to the kitchen door
Or crawling across the road on hands and knees

Just to feed the hay. Shafted by the wind,
The barrage of sleet, special delivery.

Each fencing post, mail orientated,
Skids on the envelope of black ice.

PETER TAVY

THE COOMBE

Cobbles breathing heavily
Feeling downtrodden
The small path

Brook ripple and granite barn
Taste of blackberry
Takes you by surprise

Yard full of nettles
Black corrugated iron
Still in fashion

Stout chimney smoking them out
Fern spreading sedately
Giant goose feathers

Moss, soft damp sponge
Cool green particulate
A coral reef of its own

Hazel, ash and sycamore,
Elderberry, oak and medlar
Delicate forest re-colonising

Fruit of the valley
Log stack, budleia
Dark pools, shadow's worth

A stream in harness -
Beneath the footbridge
The fern has complete mastery

Pools reflecting electricity lines
Upside down
Where you would least expect them

Pondskaters and water boatmen
Whose precise circular ripples
Punctuate the stillness

Crotchets and semi-quavers
On the water's face
Small submerged steps

Hazelnuts in tutus
Sloes like cannonballs
Grey clouds – the pigeon sky

The brook a bright ribbon
Running helter skelter
Through the maze of rocks

A glass castle
Cascading down the mountain
Delicate leaves of ash

Through which the sun
Pokes his fingers
Moorland at last

Resurrection of ancient walls
Buzzard on patrol
Fungi springs to mind

As if from outer space
Overnight
White turrets blinking

Gorse has its own place
Faint murmurings
Of vanilla

The turf as supple
As a young girl
Running downhill

Small enclosed tight knit
Communities
Lichen on a boulder gray

Outcrops of words
Deeply embedded
Fermenting on the horizon

Dartmoor lurking at my back
The sound of the brook
Shaving the bracken

Bleat of lamb,
Slowly making the grade
Brent Tor – a shark's fin

Rock like an old man's nose
A single rowanberry winks at me
Landscape swallows itself.

MIST

At times the white shroud
Has you guessing,
Circles are not impossible

You use your ears and eyes
And register small changes
In rock patterns and lichen growth.

Small streams and tracks
Become thin threads
Upon which your hopes are pinned.

You look at sheep
And wonder whether
You have met before.

WIND

The wind slices through you
Cleaves the granite,
Leaves quarries asunder,

An invisible shadow that carries itself
Across the moor in the time
It takes a rabbit to wash its face.

You head into the wind again,
Gain the lee of an old wall.
The land shivers in little ripples

The sheep are silent
They look you in the eye
As one of them.

HAIL

Hail has its own verticality
The ricochet of confetti
Dancing on the corrugated iron roof

A machine gun that gathers pace
Evolves its own guerrilla tactics
And then melts away into the undergrowth.

AMMIL

Winter's mantle, the glass cage
Crystal chandelier
That shakes in the wind

Fractures the silence
Ice in its own world
Under moonlight preens itself.

DE VALERA 'SEWS MAIL BAGS'
DARTMOOR PRISON 1916-1917

Born in New York, saved by the skin of his teeth,
And raised in Limerick, the 'long fellow'
Did time on the Moor, his studies of mathematics
And differential equations, no doubt stood him
In good stead, to weigh up the probability
Of his narrow escape from the firing squad.

'Sewing mail bags' not such a bad option after all.
Art or craft? Appropriate, in the circumstances
Considering how the Dublin Post Office went up in smoke
Well sorted and stamped its date mark on history.
Unexpected, the Easter Uprising, the surrender
And he, in charge of Boland's Flour Mill,

No doubt the price of bread went up that week,
Could just as easily have been Jacob's biscuit factory,
St Stephens, the Four Courts or the South Dublin Union
The problem, not enough guns, Cousin Wilhelm a little wary.
Shades of Roger Casement in Tralee Bay, the missed rendezvous.
And the 'Norwegian' ship scuttled with a German crew.

De Valera must have felt the draught of those bullets
In Kilmainham Jail. Last minute reprieve, penal servitude.
Then grumbled away inside Dartmoor, and with time upon his hands,
Wrote several letters to his Irish mother, asked her about his father.
Spanish, Cuban or American? The artist/sculptor/piano teacher
Who 'died' of TB in Denver, Colorado or was it Santa Fe?

ESCAPE

The first you knew about it
Would be the road blocks
Barbed wire barricades temporarily
Strung out across the road in the mist.

Police would peer into your car
Shine torches into the back
Make you open the boot
To see if you were harbouring fugitives.

Then wave you on. Prisoners always chose
The thickest mist to give them an advantage
But more often than not it led them astray..
"Were they dangerous?" we would often ask

As the window was wound down.
Alsatians straining on the leash
Stern granite faces of warders in blue.
His parting words. "They never get far".

CIRCLING

Raven black and calling
Circling above the granite
The carcase of the tor laid out
Bare, worthy of appraisal

Sweeping the ground with a keen eye
Calling the frost to heel,
Wing tip glistens in the early sun
Deeper black, the inner territory

Stands out starkly against
Dry subtle duns of brown bracken
Deep throaty call that reverberates
As a regiment of highland cattle graze the skyline.

CROSSING

Clapper bridge yawns
Marvels at its own simplicity
Fish dart under pillars
Engineering the past

Stepping stones
Set like diamonds
A necklace drawn tight
Over the river's throat

A peat pass
The jobbers track
Ponies weighed down
Find their footing.

From one side to the other
A habit, noting down
A writer's thoughts
Worth recording, the Crossing point.

CROCKERN TOR
– THE TINNERS' PARLIAMENT

They gathered in all weathers, beneath sharp skies
Debated the stars and streams of tin,
Rough homespun laws, grievances and claims,

The common sense which steered each destiny
Within the history of that metal, the hub.
Four paths at least, and a fifth from the north west,

Centered on this crossing point like spokes
Of a giant cartwheel, the land of the Dart,
A rich valley coursing with hope, rabbits and salmon.

Digging deeper there is always a rich vein
Wedged between scattered rocks
Windswept outlines engrained on memory,

A reminder of sturdy men, independent and resourceful
Firm fists of grey flecked granite in their cheeks,
They refined and cast the ingots of tradition,

Their brows returning, furrowed by the wind,
Their saddles stirruped and surviving the bog.
Relentlessly the weather taps on their shoulder.

VILLAGE OAK

The village lives inside the tree,
Dining in the dark hollow
Turves stacked in their favour
Dancing in the branches

Rough bark stretches back a thousand years,
Horses tethered outside the church house.
Propped up, the old oak leans
With dignity, green around the gills

Weddings, acorns and funerals
Parishioners pass me, one by one,
The moor tucked in under their belt
My own baptism at this granite font.

WILD BOAR AT BURRATOR

Snuffling the dark,
Strange tourists hugging the woods

Going south in winter
No doubt sniffed the acorns

From a great distance.
Meavy Oak Fair

On a spit. Local food.
Habeas Porcus.

UNEXPLODED SHELLS

We would pick these up quite regularly,
Usually spent mortar rounds
Or machine gun bullets,
Clusters of spent cartridges.

Left in the heather
Like grouse droppings.
The belts and clips
Which we could fit together.

Sometimes there were larger shells
Pom poms from the Boer war
Which got the fire arms squad
And Bomb Disposal interested.

Amazing what you could pick up
In antique shops or the homes of old soldiers
The Hales bomb, a hand grenade from
Old Exeter Street was pretty good.

A First World War survivor
Who had to defuse his own.
The detonator lasted seventy years
And when foot and mouth came

We would dig bullets out of the butts
Down Crowndale, melt the lead
And sell it to the scrap merchants
Under the old railway bridge.

VIGO BRIDGE

Once in a storm the river
At our back door rose
Eight feet in as many hours

And carried a yellow concrete mixer
With its scaffolding at least a mile
Downstream. This impressed us no end.

As did the gurgling noise of
The peaty brown torrents,
That cut a dashing swirl

Before sliding through
The old granite arches that
Connected us with the town

A flood of biblical proportions
That lived on in our imaginations.
And as we walked to school

Along the banks of the river
Beside the old monastery
We would spot the concrete mixer

Marvel at the power of water
And the watch for salmon.
Of the scaffolding there was no trace.

VIRTUOUS LADY

Above clear green salmon pools,
Slewed and walled up,
The entrance below a small cliff,
The world's chasm yawns,
A theatre door upon a stage
Where every inch of watery darkness
Is known and measured,
An aladdin's cave that comes alive
With every breath of light
As the Virtuous Lady's jewels bedecked
Outshine even Elizabeth's own crown,
Minerals in such profusion
That the colours bewitched the miners.

Fools gold and cassiterite,
Siderite and arsenical pyrite,
Titanium dioxide, Lady's Slipper
And anastase, to name but a few
Green, blue and reddish hues and tones
Nature's own crystals, recalcitrant glow worms
That shimmer in the waving torchbeams.
A feeling of reverence as if the fuse had just been lit
The smell of black powder lingering still.

Miss Oxenford, daughter of the last mine captain
Did not suffer fools gladly,
Even had her father's revolver
To keep law and order underground.

DISTRICT NURSE

She had the whole of South West Dartmoor
As her parish or so it seemed,
Indicating a degree of commitment
Her green Morris Minor eventually traded in
For a sodding great blue Volvo.
The gun dogs needed a charabang.

Every day she studied the intricacies of
Family relationships, plotted them out
On the day's chart. Dressings here
And confidences there, party to all the
Deep gossip, injecting humour
Applying poultices to grieving souls.

The real nitty-gritty of the moor
Keeping tabs on those that survived the war,
Or the tyranny of small farms
Eking out their last days under tin roofs.
She held the moor in her hands
And woe betide you, if you ever went adrift.

AUTUMN TEIGN

The valley is filled with gold
Copper leaves that punch the light

Burnished bronze shields that fuel the sky
A sea that dances above the river

A tide of beech that catches you unawares
Each slender tree anchored into autumn.

TED HUGHES
1930 - 1998

Angular, granular
Dark and brooding,
His granite brow and jaw

Presiding
Over the valley
Of the English language.

A fistful of Yorkshire
Tamed by a Devon river,
Velvet in an iron grasp,

Each line glinting in the rain,
Taut like barbed wire,
On open moorland

Hawk-sharp and sleek
Like a salmon, his inner eye
Jumping swift rapids.

WINTER AGAIN

They measure their lives out
Not in teaspoons and cappuccinos
But in blizzards, buckrakes and bad winters.

If your animals survive
There is some satisfaction in that,
A bond, forged on the weather's anvil.

Outposts of humanity
Living in the eye of the moor
Shouldering it like a side of bacon

That lives above the kitchen table
Hoisted high up on an old door
With a sack of flour and cheese

Tethered on a pulley, out of range of cats and dogs,
Rats and children. For emergencies only.
You never know quite when it is coming back.

LAST WORD   UNDER MOONLIGHT

The moor glitters   shrugs its shoulders
Sires the odd stream   spawns a river or two
Language of ripple   teasing the bank.
Sheaf of ruffled water   strides down towards the sea.
Sheds a tear of granite   has a bath in the peat
Wallows in its own watershed   throws in the sponge.

NOTES

THE MOOR: This is of course Dartmoor not Exmoor or Broadmoor. The history of the moor involves Venville rights, Quartermen, Lydford Assizes, The Duchy of Cornwall, stannary towns, coinage, tin mining, copper mining, pony drifts and snow drifts, prisoners and convicts, cattle grids and ice creams, blowing houses, and quarries, reservoirs, peat cutting, swaling, jobbers paths, army training, live firing, sheep rustling, beef cattle, rabbit warrens and pixies. Dartmoor is an extraordinarily beautiful area of wildness which gives enormous pleasure to many people even if all they do is just drive across it. My own favourite time is winter when the snow is down and you can walk to many places you cannot normally get to, the light is sometimes fantastic.

THE BAD WINTER: This was the 1962- 63 winter. The snow started falling on 29th December and with subsequent heavy falls of snow, the frosts lasted right through January, February into early March. With temperatures as low as -15° C it was the coldest prolonged winter since 1740. The winter of 1947 had more snow but was not as cold. In terms of snowfall the Great Blizzard of March 1891 was even more extreme and then there were snow drifts 80 feet deep in Tavy Cleave that didn't disappear till late in the summer. These bad winters are still talked about even now. For me the winter of 1962-63 left a deep and wonderful impression, a great white space and an addictive silence.

BLIZZARD: Snow had come on Boxing Day but it came with a vengeance on the evening of Saturday 29th December 1962. Dr Beeching had it in for the Great Western Railway line that ran through Tavistock South. Living as we did in Mount Tavy Road, Tavistock, we used to hear every train go through as it went north towards Lydford and then veered off towards Launceston. In the other direction the line went to Yelverton and Plymouth. We heard the last train go through as it was snowing heavily. One train got stuck at Bickleigh and had to be abandoned. Another goods train on the Southern

Region line was buried near Lydford and the two ancient locomotives with snow ploughs sent out to rescue them also got stuck on Sourton Down. The inspector in charge was called Edgar Snow. Indeed trains seemed to get stuck on exposed stretches of the track quite regularly and had to be dug out by hand sometimes by hundreds of men. This often took days. Snow plough rains were getting stuck in February as well. These snow plough locomotives were built in the 1890s and were joined together back to back, and they often charged the snow drift to break through. These class 700 locomotives known as 'Black Motors' should really have been in a museum. One interesting point is that steam trains were much better at defrosting points than diesels which of course had no steam. Some steam trains were brought back into service for these months.

CHILDE'S TOMB: This is on the edge of Foxtor Mire south east of Princetown and well marked. The story so much as can be determined is that Childe, a young but wealthy Saxon was out hunting when he got caught out on his own in a fierce blizzard. Before he died he left a note or some message saying that he would leave all his Plymstock estates to whoever found his body and gave him a Christian burial. Tavistock Abbey claimed him but the good people of Plymstock Priory lay in wait to ambush the body or so it is said. The monks built a temporary bridge over the Tavy and so secured the body and the inheritance. Pity about the horse. There is a cross on Foxtor Mire commemorating the man and his demise.

TAVISTOCK ABBEY: This was an early but wealthy Benedictine abbey with lands in Devon, Cornwall and Dorset, founded by Ordulph in 981. The Abbey was sacked in a Viking raid in 997 and was rebuilt soon afterwards. In 1114 it was given a priory in the Isles of Scilly. In 1209 on the 8th of May, 112 pirates were beheaded on Tresco, which gives some idea of the scale of the problems faced by shipping. Tavistock Abbey also had a cider press at Plymstock and brought the cider in large pipes (wooden casks holding 110 gallons) up the Tavy to Morwellham and then inland for consumption. The monks also used fish weirs to catch salmon. By 1518 Tavistock also had its own printing press, the only other presses in the country were at Westminster, Oxford, St Albans, London, York and Cambridge. After the dissolution of the abbey in 1539 no more books were printed in Devon for 150 years. For more details see *Tavistock Abbey* by H.P.R.Finberg.

ARCHAEOLOGY – THE LYDFORD PENNY: In 1966 and 1967 there were excavations at Lydford by Dr Peter Addyman and students from Queen's University Belfast to explore the Saxon village of Lydford. Basically this entailed some test trenches around the earlier Motte and Bailey castle as well as digging up the car park of the Lydford Inn. Food yards not food miles. Sadly although an important mint in Saxon times, no Lydford pennies turned up during the dig. Like Tavistock, Lydford suffered in 997 from the Viking raid and there was much slaughter. This was recorded in the Anglo Saxon Chronicle. Many Lydford pennies are however to be found in Sweden and in particular the island of Gotland in the Baltic. For two or three weeks I was allowed to work alongside the students and developed more than a passing interest in history and archaeology. One day an old Rolls Royce turned up and out got Ralegh Radford the eminent Devon archaeologist, just to see how things were going. In Saxon times Lydford was the most populous place in Devon after Exeter. The parish of Lydford takes in most of Dartmoor and many people were incarcerated in its bleak Norman castle. The famous epitaph to a watchmaker is in the churchyard.

TAVISTOCK MARKET: Self explanatory, details from Finberg op. cit. Fridays and farmers' markets not much different these days.

NEXT SPRING: Sadly thousands of sheep died on the moor during the 1962-'63 winter and their bones often lay scattered to the four winds. This was then followed by Foot and Mouth in 1967 when the moor was closed off for public access. Escaped convicts were quite a common occurrence.

ZACHARIAS PASCOE: 1749 – 1843, born and married in Wendron near Helston in Cornwall, Zacharias Pascoe moved up to Stoke Damerel and

Plymouth Dock in 1772. He was a tin streamer and eventually worked on the moor, where he lived for at least 50 years. He 'came to fame' as the leader of the Chagford Tinners' Riot of 1793. Later he built himself a cottage and a dug a small well near Rundlestone. In 1841 he is recorded as living at Merrivale aged 92 and recorded in the census as a tin miner. He was also my great-great-great-great grandfather and I am indebted to Dr Tom Greeves for information about his activities concerning riots and enclosure. He had sons, grandsons and great grandsons all called Zacharias Pascoe so it must have been a bit confusing. They preferred to stay above ground and were stone masons living near Wheal Lucky which was a small mine near Rundlestone. Reputedly this mine produced a small amount of gold, enough to make a wedding ring for a minor Royal.

THE CHAGFORD TINNERS' RIOT: This occurred on 12th November 1793 and is fairly well documented and was brought to my attention by Dr Tom Greeves. It seems that the Cornish miners felt that their two friends had been unfairly imprisoned, riotous behaviour was 'quite normal' in Cornwall. What is far more likely to have happened is that they had just been paid. Often with the tribute system men were only paid quarterly in arrears, which meant that when they were paid it was cause for celebration, and like the navvies they were a law unto themselves. The gang of miners numbered about 17 or 18, though others may have dispersed before they reached the magistrates house in Cheriton Bishop. Zacharias Pascoe's name with three children headed the list, he was also the oldest man there and had, like some of the others, come up from the Helston area 25 years previously, when there was a slump in the copper prices. Many of the mines in West Devon were worked by Cornish men. Wendron was an area particularly given to surface tin streaming and much of the Dartmoor was also streamed for tin. Zacharias must have liked it on the moor. The mine he would have been working at near the Warren House Inn was Vitifer and Birch Tor. Zacharias died in October 1843 aged 94. Chagford is still standing and has prospered. Very chic these days.

Leat: These small man-made streams are a vital part of the moorland system providing power to blowing houses and mines as well as water to Plymouth and Devonport. One leat on the southern moor from the Plym still provides water for the china clay industry at Lee Moor. They are small marvels of engineering and have to contour round slopes in some pretty inhospitable places. Leats from the Tavy also provide power for two hydro-electric schemes, one at Mary Tavy and the other following the course of the old Tavistock canal to Morwellham on the Tamar.

Moor Rain: Dartmoor is one of the wettest places in southern England and Princetown often has more than 80 inches a year. Without the rain there would be no rivers and no peat. Dartmoor spawns many rivers, the Dart, the Tavy, the Taw, the Teign, the Plym, the Avon, the Erme, the Walkham and the Meavy just to name a few. Some of the most wonderful rivers in southern England.

Granite: Granite is a volcanic rock known in the trade as an igneous intrusion. These extinct volcanoes pushed their molten magma skywards and the weather has been eroding them ever since. Granite is very hard but often has a mixture of quartz and mica and the all important minerals within it, hence the mining, not just of tin and copper, but of lead, silver and even wolfram. Often it is the metamorphic aureole on the rim of Dartmoor which has the richest veins. West Dartmoor is essentially the same geologically as Cornwall and the lodes often cross over the border.

China Clay: This is an important feature in the south west of Dartmoor around Lee Moor, Wotter and Shaugh Prior. It is in fact anhydrous aluminium silicate made from decomposed feldspar and is often found in deep deposits. The first man to start mining it was William Cookworthy from Plymouth who discovered deposits at Tregonning Hill, near Helston in 1746 and started his porcelain works in Plymouth making teapots, plates cups and saucers. His business was later eclipsed by Josiah Wedgwood in Staffordshire. The china clay deposits are sometimes known by their

Chinese name - kaolin. The workings on Dartmoor did not start till the 1830s. China Clay is mostly used in paper to give the gloss as well as for ceramics, pharmaceuticals and cosmetics. During the 1941 blitz on Plymouth the white conical mounds of waste were a dead giveaway to German bombers on moonlit nights. Go towards Lee Moor, then left hand down a bit. The workings today dwarf the earlier workings and the waste mounds have now been stabilised with grass and trees and have sheep grazing on them. Christo; born 1935, is the Bulgarian artist who wraps buildings to make large scale artistic installations.

FICE'S WELL: This well is not far from Rundlestone three fields in and was constructed by John Fitz of Tavistock in 1568 after he was caught out in a mist with his wife and led astray by pixies. He drank from the well and all at once he found his bearings. The well apparently has a curative effect on eye complaints and is well worth visiting.

FRENCH PRISONERS: During the Napoleonic War French prisoners were often kept on hulks, usually captured French vessels and many of these prisoners were left languishing below decks in the Hamoaze. The idea to build a prison at Princetown to hold 5,000 prisoners evolved in 1805. The prison was built using mainly Cornish stone masons and finally completed in 1809. The first 2,500 prisoners were marched up there in May 1809, a long bedraggled group of men hauling their own luggage. A month or two later the prison population had doubled to 5,000. At times this was again doubled to 10,000, and with an influx of rowdy American prisoners in 1812 the conditions were very cramped indeed. Many of the French officers were given parole and lived in local towns and lived the life of O'Reilly by comparison. Nearly all of them respected this trust and it must have been an extraordinary time. Twinning with a difference.

Interestingly not all of the 'French' prisoners were French. Elisabeth Stanbrook in her recent book on Dartmoor War Prison says that there were many from the Dutch East Indies, Malays, Chinese and Eurasians as well as Spaniards, Germans, Italians, Swiss, Prussians, Poles, Austrians as well as

Belgians, Dutch, Swedes and Africans. Many gambled away everything including their clothes and were left naked and destitute in the lofts living like animals. These were *Les Romains*. Some became very respectable citizens in later life, even lawyers.

However, during the War of 1812, the American officers were not accorded the same privileges of parole. But a quirk of clerical efficiency allowed English sailors who had gone over to the American side to claim any prize money due to them whilst serving with the British Navy. Conditions in the prison were far from ideal and the bread was continually adulterated, which led to riots, like watered down porridge in later years. In one incident in 1815, seven American prisoners were shot dead and 34 injured.

In January 1814 the prison was cut off by a blizzard, the snow drifting as high as the fourteen foot walls. The frost lasted right through till 20th March. There are large cemeteries for both French and American prisoners who died of exhaustion, fever, typhus, dysentery and other causes whilst in prison.

PASCOE'S WELL: This well still exists alongside the road near Princetown under a canopy of granite, looking rather like a Dartmoor dog kennel or a large milk churn stand. There is still water inside but it is rather silted up and needs a bit of clearing round. Arthur Smith at Rundlestone says he used it in the bad winter of 1962-63 to get water for animals so it must have been free of ice in the coldest of weathers, very useful indeed. And no doubt it holds water in summer during a drought. It was built by Zacharias Pascoe in about 1806 and named after him. This was the same time that work started on building the prison and he must have been present when the first prisoners came in.

PASCOE'S COTTAGE: This is the cottage that went with the well. The two being in many ways interlinked. The cottage would have been built by Zacharias himself and may well have been the subject of an encroachment order of 1806 in Walkhampton records. But there was no fine recorded and

Zacharias stayed put. He had obviously found a small piece of 'No Man's Land' between the Duchy of Cornwall and the Maristow estates. He was allowed to stay and the cottage features on a sale map of Tor Royal in 1828 with his name *Z Pascoe* written across the map. Zachary was also consulted about boundaries by the Maristow estates from time to time. The prison leat ran nearby and Zacharias may well have had a supervisory role being a tin streamer. There was also a mine nearby called Wheal Lucky. Pascoe's cottage existed until the 1960s and was used by the prison officers for accommodation. You can just make out the low walls which have been incorporated within the field wall. Like many buildings on the moor it only exists today on old maps, old photographs and in people's memories.

CONVICTS ON THE MOVE: It used to be fairly common to see convicts on the move between the prison and the quarry or on the farm, or on their way out to do a spot of tree planting or dry stone wall building. They used to be accompanied by a warder on horseback. Dog handlers came in during the 1970s but after 30 years they have been disbanded. Sadly the prison farm was wound down and eventually closed in August 2004 when the animals were sold at a dispersal sale. Usually it was a privilege to work outside, not a punishment, though working in the quarry could be very hard work in all weathers. Most men working outside had only 18 months to go till the end of their sentence, so the incentive to escape was greatly reduced.

The prison farm was a great success story enclosing more and more land. It grew hay, turnips, mangold wurzels, Belgian carrots, barley, oats, vetches and even flax. In one year the prisoners built 8,000 yards of new walls. By 1864 the farm was producing 7,217 gallons of milk, 286 lbs of butter, 326 cwt of cabbage, 49 cwt of onions and 159 cwt of turnips. At its peak in 1891 the Dartmoor Prison Farm covered more than 2,000 acres and employed 1,000 prisoners.

PEAT CUTTING: This has now stopped. This particular scene was near Pew Tor in the 1960s. The main problem with peat cutting was drying the peat and getting it off the moor. At one time it was an industry and near

Rattlebrook there was a peat works and a railway. In the 19th century, Dartmoor prison had its own naptha works to light the prison and the prisoners dug nearly 2,000 tons of peat in one year. In medieval times when the wood ran out peat was turned into charcoal to give a good heat for smelting the tin ore. On Dartmoor the peats are called turves and the bank, a tie. Drying the peat in a wet summer was always a problem. If you cut the peat too large it never dried out, too small, it fell apart.

SWALING AT ERME PLAINS: This was in the 1970s when swaling was still common practice. It was a great skill to burn enough grass and not too much. If the fires got out of control they could burn for weeks. The fresh grass underneath the heather was always good for sheep and kept the heather under control. Quartermen are the cattlemen who each have a quarter of the moor to supervise when cattle would be driven up for the summer grazing. Cattle would come from great distances, even from the south coast. Then in return, sheep might be grazed down in the lowlands in winter. A good example of transhumance and shared grazing patterns. For instance Hubert Snowdon's cattle came up from Thurlestone on the coast every summer onto the moor and sheep from Dartmoor came down onto his farm in winter for lambing and then improved his own pasture.

DITSWORTHY WARREN: This warren is famous on Dartmoor as it was the largest and was worked till 1954. I first heard about it from George Bowden who lived next door to my grandparents in Meavy. George had worked there from the age of eight and so his warrening career must have started around 1897. It was his aunt old Mrs Ware, or Old Lady Ware as she was known, who lived out there, and like his brother Harry Bowden, George was sent out there to work but more importantly to keep his cousin Percy Ware company. In the 1901 census it shows Percy aged 10 and George Bowden aged 11. Mrs Emmeline Ware is shown as the warrener and in Sheepstor, George's father Robert is shown as a road contractor. George lived out at Ditsworthy but for the census was back in Sheepstor. The 1901 census show that two warren labourers and game keepers from Cornwood called Phillips were employed as well. George's elder brother, Ernest Bowden aged 18, is shown as a tin miner almost certainly working at Kit tin mine in Sheepstor.

GEORGE BOWDEN: George was born on 15th December 1889 at Pitts Cottage just behind the church at Sheepstor, the youngest of eleven children. His family came from Brisworthy near Cadover in the parish of Meavy and they had been farmers out there since Elizabethan times. His mother Caroline Tuke Andrews came from Meavy itself. At one time they had run the Royal Oak but obviously there was more money in building the roads. I knew George and his wife Ethel Smale very well indeed. It was always a highlight of the visit to go and talk to them. It was here that I heard many of the stories about Dartmoor. George had a long but hard working life. He took great pride in his job as village lengthsmen, keeping the parish lanes neat and tidy and was heartbroken when he had to give up in 1955 after he had done the job for 30 years. He knew every ditch and hedge for miles around, and in winter kept the snow off the roads. During the First World War he served on board *HMS Cumberland*, an old county cruiser. She had 31 Bellville boilers, which were notoriously difficult to service under pressure. Shovelling coal in a bunker was often more dangerous than working in a mine, as the coal could shift at any moment and in a storm you could easily get buried alive. China clay was also important and provided much work locally. Redlake is right out in the middle of the moor and men would only return at weekends. The drying sheds were hot and filled with steam as the china clay was compressed and then ready for bagging up. Fernworthy reservoir near Chagford was built in 1937 to supply extra water for Torquay and Paignton. The snow storm that George and his brother Harry were caught out in was on Christmas Eve 1899. Not quite as bad as 1891 but almost as bad. The snow lasted till March. They were both lucky to survive. Harry Bowden later worked on the Edgcumbe estate at Maker and at Cothele. He survived the trenches and then went out to America as a gamekeeper and is buried alongside the Ohio River.

YEO FARM: This is just up from Marchant's Cross and for me was always one of the loveliest of farm houses on the southern edge of the moor. Sadly it was derelict for many years and has only recently been brought into the 21st century. What also interested me was that this was where Ethel Smale lived here during the First World War. She was born in Clearbrook and later married George Bowden in May 1920. The story of the train whistle always seemed particularly evocative. Her brother Jack and George met by chance on the Menin Road and both came back in one piece. Jack was very keen on motorbikes. The railway line to Princetown was closed in 1955. Ethel Smale was born in 1891 and died in 1985 at the ripe old age of 94. I last saw her in the July that year and she was still reciting her own poem about Meavy and waxing lyrical about the village. She was a very good friend of my grandmother's and they used to put on Shakespeare plays in the village hall during the 1950s. Ethel also made real clotted cream and junket. She was very intelligent and should really have been a teacher. She had a close association with the school and the class would often visit her in her house to hear about local history.

BURRATOR AT DUSK: The building of the Burrator dam in the 1890s was a vast undertaking in Sheepstor parish. Its main aim was to supply more water for Plymouth. As far back as the 16th century Sir Francis Drake had built a leat which still bears his name today. When they built the dam farmland and houses had to be flooded and George Bowden was one of the few people I knew who remembered what it was like before it was submerged. In the 1950s when there was a drought Ethel Bowden and my grandmother walked on the bed of the reservoir and inspected Sheepstor bridge. George was very keen to hear what the pointing was like as he had done it as a small boy. The pointing was still in good shape and hadn't been leached out. George was pleased.

BURRATOR AND THE LUFTWAFFE: May 19th 1941 - George Bowden and Harold Shillibeer were on duty that night, Harold worked for the reservoir water treatment plant. Curiously enough there was no heavy raid on

Plymouth that night. The main blitz had been on the nights 20-22 March and 21-30 April 1941. Water was critical for fire fighting so Burrator was a key target. Also it was very visible on a clear night and it was no coincidence that searchlights were placed on Lynch Common and Roborough Down.

What actually happened is still open to speculation. It may have been a reconnaissance flight. The names of the German aircrew were Paul Nowacki, Joachim Kasten, Hans Knor and Gunther Hitschfeld. Their bodies were later taken to Cannock Chase to be buried at the German war cemetery in the 1960s. The Junkers 88 was a very good aircraft often used as a night fighter but could be used as a bomber or even as a torpedo aircraft.

THE GARDEN NEXT DOOR: This garden belonged to George Bowden and was next door to my grandparents who lived at The White Cottage in Meavy. There was a small stone stile that we clambered over between the two gardens and we were always going backwards and forwards. George kept a wonderful garden and was always there if he wasn't out trimming hedgerows. I remember his raspberries and the red flowers on the runner beans. George and Ethel had one son, David, but David never married so my brother and I were, I suspect, the next best thing to grandchildren and we would always go over for tea and spend just as long there as at our own grandparent's house. It was the stories about the moor and the village that were so fascinating. The German helmet still exists but the valances of the Sherman tank which he picked up off Callisham Down have gone to the scrap yard.

CAPTAIN HENRY – THE WHITE COTTAGE: This was my grandparents' house in Meavy. Captain Henry, or Captain Moulton as he was known locally. had been on convoys in both wars and had served most of his life on P&O liners. In about 1967 he got the charts out and showed my brother and I some of the things he was up to during the war. He mentioned a particular convoy where nine ships were torpedoed over three nights by a U boat pack. A few years ago I managed to deduce which convoy it was: OB 318 from a few cryptic marks in his diary. i.e. 'Dep Ryk' and 'A Hx' which meant 'Depart Reykjavik and 'Arrive Halifax'. His vessel was *HMS Ranpura* a converted Armed Merchant Cruiser, sister ship to the *HMS Rawalpindi*, which went down in the Iceland Gap in Nov 1939. Another sister ship *HMS Rajputana* was torpedoed in April 1941 in the Denmark Straits. What is interesting about the convoy OB318 is that the escorts managed to bring one U Boat to surface, U 110. The enigma machine and officer codes were secretly retrieved and rushed down to Bletchley Park which gave them vital information for cracking the Enigma code. My grandfather of course could not talk about this but he must have known that a U boat was brought to surface and boarded. In his own way he was giving us clues, which I have now been able to follow up. He had many narrow escapes in the North Atlantic and in the Pacific.

LAST OF THE BLUE GRASS: This is in a sense the life of David Bowden who at the time of writing is still living in Meavy. David was born in 1930 and was in the REME as a national serviceman. The earthquake was of course Cephalonia in 1953, featured in Louis de Bernieres book *'Captain Correlli's Mandolin'* now made into a film. The things David saw left a deep impression on his mind. The Drake connection is a little obscure but it is through the Crymes family I believe. Meavy Barton was for many years known as Drake Manor. Joan Strode, who was the daughter of Sir William Strode who lived at Meavy Barton, married Sir Francis Drake (1588-1637) whose father Sir Thomas Drake was brother to the more famous pirate (1540-1595). He died of dysentery and was buried at sea in Nombre Dios bay in Puerto Rico.

David got his name 'Buster' from antics in the Walkhampton school playground when he stood up to the school bully, the name stuck. Growing up during the war with all the American troops around in 1944 Buster was fascinated by their music, the jazz and was even listening to central European music at Plaster Down camp above Horrabridge when DP's, (displaced persons), were housed there after the war. Russian, Polish and

Czech music was common. He would sometimes go into Plymouth and stand outside the Polish club near North Road station to listen to the music. He loved Stephan Grappelli and Django Reinhardt, in fact David likes all music from Bach to Boogie and formed his locally famous band, 'Buster Bowden and the Western Revellers'. They would travel around performing in the 1960s and 70s. He has played in Dartmoor Prison, Devonport, Tavistock and Exeter University. David is keen on family history and still talks about one of his ancestors, Dicky Boy Pengelly from Brisworthy. One of his other relatives, one of the Pettigrews, actually died on the Doom Bar, in the Camel estuary, near Padstow as a life boatman at about the same time as the American Civil war, so whenever he is in the pub, David makes as a point of having a pint of Sharp's Doom Bar to remember him. In his day job, David was an electrician with SWEB in Plymouth and had a penchant for motorbikes, his favourite being the Matchless. The refrains come from Sir Henry Newbolt's famous poem 'Drakes's Drum' which is now kept over the hill in Buckland Abbey.

POSTMAN: This is based on an interview with Arthur Smith of Rundlestone who was postman in the Postbridge and Yelverton area for many years. He has lived in the same house since he was born and has seen some bad weather up there particularly in 1947 and of course 1962-63. Arthur used to deliver post to a good friend of mine the photographer Chris Chapman, when he was living at Powder Mills in the 1970s.

PETER TAVY – THE COMBE: This is the wonderful hidden valley that runs up past the old school and chapel and was written on a poetry workshop given by Roselle Angwin, combined with a print workshop by Mary Gillett.

MIST: To navigate in the mist can be a real problem particularly if the compass is playing up. Even to drive across the moor at night in mist needs a high degree of care. Animals however know the ground so well they can always re-orientate themselves.

WIND: Wind on Dartmoor if it is coming from the south west can be evil. The question always is what is it bringing with it. The combination of rain or snow or sleet can make conditions very bleak indeed. Wind turbines would generate a fair few mega-watts on the moor…

HAIL: Hailstorms can be particularly vicious on the moor. In some instances you are well advised to take shelter if possible. Animals seem almost oblivious to it.

AMMIL: This a peculiar Dartmoor term which should not be confused with hoar frost. Both however are very beautiful. Ammil is the effect when a thaw starts and then rain freezes over branches, trees and plants but it forms a thin sheen of ice rather than frost crystals. Sometimes the effect lasts for hours and at others for days on end. The term ammil is thought to come from the Saxon word 'ammel', which then became enamel.

DE VALERA 'SEWS MAIL BAGS': Eamon de Valera 1882-1975 was a contradictory man, a rugby-playing mathematician who liked religion and narrowly missed being executed by firing squad after the Easter Uprising in 1916. Born in New York he was raised in Limerick by his mother's family. Traces of his father are very sketchy indeed and there appears to be no marriage certificate. On his birth certificate his father is called Vivion de Valera and his mother Catherine or Kate Coll. It is unclear whether his father was actually an American citizen and he may well have been Cuban. When Eamon is two, his father dies of TB on the way to Denver, Colorado but there is no death or marriage certificate.

The Easter uprising started on 24th April 1916 and lasted about a week. De Valera commanded the 3rd Batallion which held Boland's Flour Mill. In seven days' fighting 550 people were killed and more than 2,000 wounded. Some say that de Valera suffered a nervous breakdown during this time. After the surrender he was court-martialled and sentenced to death, his sentence eventually being commuted to penal servitude for life. He was sent to Dartmoor Prison with 65 other Irish rebels including Harry Boland, Dr

Richard Hayes and Desmond FitzGerald, father of Dr Garrett FitzGerald. The Irishmen did not integrate with the other prisoners who were mostly conscientious objectors. These three were regarded as leaders and troublemakers and were sent to Maidstone prison by train shackled to each other by their legs. De Valera threatened to go on hunger strike and was regarded as a bit of a firebrand. There is even a story that at one prison the Irish prisoners managed to persuade one gullible prison Governor that there was a special Irish festival in honour of WB Yeats and the Governor laid on a special meal for them which they rather enjoyed. Harry Boland was, incidentally, in love with Kitty Kiernan from Grannard as was the 'big fellow', Michael Collins.

What saved de Valera from the firing squad was not just his American birth, but the fact that the British Government was desperately trying to get America to join the war in Europe on their side. So de Valera was saved more by wartime politics than his place of birth. Later he became Prime Minister and then President of the Irish Republic.

ESCAPE: Escaped prisoners were a fairly common feature of daily life and if you were crossing the moor you were often held up a checkpoints on the road, usually near Rundlestone if you were coming from Tavistock. One famous incident was that of 'The Mad Axeman,' alias Frank Mitchell, who escaped on 12th December 1966. One warder I spoke to said that he was all right if you treated him fairly. He seems to have had more than the usual freedoms accorded to normal prisoners and there were rumours of him having egg and bacon brought to his cell for breakfast, visits from certain ladies and access to Tavistock when it suited him… All rumours of course, but there were worse people inside than him. Despite the mobilisation of Royal Marine Commandos he got clean away but was never seen again. His clothes and a foot long blade were discovered by a roadside thirty miles away. Many suspect that he was a victim of a gangland killing. But no one knows what actually happened to him.

Three years earlier, another escape occurred in December 1963, and the prisoner gave himself up having fallen into the lake at Mount House School and was found hiding in a cupboard in a detached house in the woods. Two masters, one, a young athletic type called Mr Gay, and the more elderly but highly intellectual, Mr Witherington, confronted the man who had hidden in a wardrobe upstairs. They simply followed the wet footprints and the prisoner gave himself up without any fuss. He also surrendered some very valuable bars of prison chocolate. We later found out that the escaped convict was called Henry Seymour Bradley, what he had done and where he came from were never divulged to us… As we were at boarding school at the time and weren't allowed out, we had a certain degree of respect for anyone who had regained his freedom, however briefly.

CIRCLING: At one time there were eagles on Dartmoor and one day they may return. Ospreys would certainly have a few salmon to pinch as long as the otters hadn't got there first. In the 19th century Rachel Evans and Mrs Bray both comment on ravens nesting on the top of Vixen Tor.

CROSSING: In the past there were many peat passes and jobbers' tracks that enabled journeymen to carry loads across the moor. Some of these still exist. Richard Hansford Worth 1868-1950 and William Crossing 1847-1928 were two very well known Dartmoor writers. Worth's *Dartmoor* and Crossing's *Dartmoor Worker* and his *Guide to Dartmoor* are still standard texts today. Clapper bridges and stepping stones are of course environmentally friendly feats of engineering.

CROCKERN TOR: This is between Two Bridges and Postbridge and was the site of the ancient Tinners Parliaments which were held on Dartmoor long before they ever held them in Cornwall… There were four stannary towns, Tavistock, Plympton, Ashburton and Chagford with Lydford as the main jail and seat of administration. The tinners met and discussed their own matters, ie assay, coinage, survey, rights, tin bounds and setts etc. They held court and were a law unto themselves like robber barons. In 1198 Cornish tinners and Devon tinners separated and held their courts at different times. Tin had to be stamped within 14 days of smelting and tax or coinage taken.

The earliest complete records are for a Parliament held in 1494 and 24 representatives came from each town. And they had to be there at 8am. There were ten sittings between 1494 and 1703. The last full Parliament was held at Crockern Tor in 1749. They must have been extraordinary events. This poem was written in 1994 to commemorate the 500th anniversary.

VILLAGE OAK: This is of course the tree known as the Royal Oak at Meavy which was old in the time of Queen Elizabeth I. It may well be around 950 years old and as they say known to King John and the hunt... It is so large that people have dined inside the trunk and even in the branches, dancing on a kind of platform... It is the fourth largest oak in Devon and the oldest on Dartmoor by a long chalk. It has been propped up from time to time. The Royal Oak pub has the curious distinction of still being a Church House owned by the parish and the rents go to help pay the parish rates. It was a place of refreshment for the farmers who came to church on horseback from far out on the moor. Meavy Oak Fair held in June is always a special time and I remember going to it many times as a child. My parents were married in the church and I was baptised there. Both my grandparents' funerals were held there. So from an early age the oak, the green and the pub were key features in my life.

WILD BOAR AT BURRATOR: A few years ago wild boar were photographed near Burrator. They had been let loose on the edge of Exmoor and had slowly made their way south, the oak woods below Sheepstor are steep and private enough for their guzzling. This poem first appeared in *'Open Mouthed'* published by Prospect Books of Totnes in 2006. I am sure the wild boar are still around, they have been seen on the moor just above Horrabridge and in the woods near Samford Spiney. If they are not careful they will end up on a spit at Meavy Oak Fair.

UNEXPLODED SHELLS: My brother Roger had a particular penchant for weapons, guns, gun cartridges and shell cases. Sometimes they were still armed and the detonators were often live. There was at least one visit to Tavistock Police station and I think the bomb squad were called out. They were very understanding. The Pom Pom shells from the Boer War were I think still alive, as were some of the rounds from Dartmoor. His real treasure was a Hales Bomb from 1914, a forerunner of the Mills bomb given to him by Sgt Grylls in Tavistock. The foot and mouth outbreak was in 1967 when the moor was closed down for military training. The lead obtained from melting down the spent rounds was sold to the scrap merchant in Mount Tavy Road and the price reflected the going rate for lead on the world market.

VIGO BRIDGE: Built in 1773 this was very close to where we lived at 11 Mount Tavy Road in the 1960s. It gave access to the main town. The house backed on to the river and it was always touch and go in a flash flood as the bridge held the water back. The Tavy is the second fastest river in the country after the Spey and races down to the sea. In spate it had no respect for builder's equipment and the whole set of scaffolding and mixer disappeared overnight and ended up at the far end of the meadows. From here it was a wonderful walk to school in Plymouth road past the salmon leap and the old abbey walls.

VIRTUOUS LADY MINE: This was at Double Waters where the Tavy and the Walkham meet. It was an Elizabethan copper mine that was started in 1588 and worked till 1807. Opened again in 1830 it closed in the 1870s. In the 1960s Miss Oxenford, whose father or grandfather had been the last mine captain, would take people down, and what a wonderful experience it was. The minerals were some of the best in the country and are in the Natural History Museum in London. She even had piece of moon rock which she showed us with great pride. The mine is now walled up but was one of the most interesting in the area. It was worked to a depth of 20 fathoms and employed 43 people.

DISTRICT NURSE: Joyce Damerel lived in Buckland Monachorum, and was a real character who loved horses and gun dogs. She specialised in pointers and was a key member, with Rupert Hill, of the West Dartmoor Working Gundog Club. They knew how to enjoy themselves… She also told me about some sad cases of people who had let themselves go on the moor and believed that the end of the world was coming and did not feed themselves or their animals properly. The moor can get to you. When she wanted peace and quiet she would walk on the moor on her own. She was an excellent district nurse, didn't suffer fools gladly, called a spade a spade. She had suffered from a riding accident in her youth and had broken her back, but that never stopped her from doing a full day on the grouse moors.

AUTUMN TEIGN: This was near Dunsford where the Morris's are, the edge tool works, and quite a place that is. The technology has not changed much since the 1840s and very good their tools are too. I used to have a spar hook made by them but I gave it to a thatcher who still uses it to this day. They hold their edge, those tools, and are much sought after.

TED HUGHES: This poem was written the day he died, Thursday 29th Oct 1998 and was published in the Western Morning News a few days later. In *Moortown* Ted Hughes says that he thought Yorkshire was remote till he went to live in North Devon. Sadly his first wife Sylvia Plath committed suicide in early February 1963 during the Bad Winter. Until then they were living only a few miles from Dartmoor in North Tawton.

WINTER AGAIN: This story of the bacon and flour on a door in the kitchen was told to me by a farmer in Salcombe who had been visiting relatives on the edge of the moor and seen it on a farm near Ashburton. He said they were devils for gambling and whisky.

LAST WORD: Rivers have to start somewhere. I was born in Plymouth near the Hamoaze, started with the Meavy, then I went to school in Dartmouth, then back to the Tavy and now it is the Walkham. Rivers teach you so much.

Over the years I have consulted various books to check up on facts and these books in themselves are a rich resource of information.

A few of them are listed here:

Crossing's Guide to Dartmoor 1912

Crossing's Dartmoor Worker 1966 – originally a series of articles for the *Western Morning News* published in 1903

Dartmoor – Richard Hansford Worth 1953

Industrial Archaeology of Dartmoor – Helen Harris 1968

Tavistock Abbey – HPR Finberg 1969

The Blizzard of '91 – Clive Carter 1971

Dartmoor Prison – Rufus Rendle 1979

High Dartmoor – Eric Hemery 1983

Tin Mines and Miners of Dartmoor – Tom Greeves 1986

Dartmoor Stone – Stephen Woods 1988

A Winter Remembered – Robert E Trevelyan 1998

The Book of Meavy – Pauline Hemery 1999

Dartmoor Prison – Vol 1 & 2 Ron Joy 2002

Dartmoor's War Prison & Church 1805-1817 –
Elisabeth Stanbrook 2002